T0194861

THE LOVE
and
LIGHT FIELD

HOW TO RAISE YOUR VIBRATION

ANA LIOR

BALBOA.PRESS

A DIVISION OF HAY HOUSE

Balboa Press books may be ordered through booksellers or by contacting:

Balboa Press
A Division of Hay House
1663 Liberty Drive
Bloomington, IN 47403
www.balboapress.com
844-682-1282

Print information available on the last page.

ISBN: 978-1-9822-5921-1 (sc)
ISBN: 978-1-9822-5923-5 (hc)
ISBN: 978-1-9822-5922-8 (e)

Library of Congress Control Number: 2020923119

Balboa Press rev. date: 11/28/2020

For anyone struggling and stuck on lower frequency patterns—be it dealing with stress, struggling with guilt and shame, being afraid or apathetic—and willing to raise their frequency to move into higher emotions, those of love, peace, joy, and other high vibrational states such as enlightenment.

Would you like to live a life filled with joy, laughter, and bliss?

CONTENTS

Dear Reader,

It is such a pleasure to me that you picked up this book. I would like to thank you for wanting to raise your vibration.

Maharishi wrote the following in the book *Enlightenment to Every Individual, Invincibility to Every Nation*: "What is a bulb? It is a very small filament. How much is that in relation to the whole volume of the room? It's a very insignificant area. Yet it becomes lighted and the whole room becomes lighted. ... Like that, one person, one slightly enlightened person, is good enough for the whole society. It's a blessing for the whole society."

I therefore want to thank you for being a blessing to the whole society.

The reason I write this book is to raise the frequency of the planet and humanity one individual human at a time. I have become deeply compassionate over the past few years, after an incident where I thought I was about to die, and my mission, like so many others' on this planet in this day and age, is to awaken humanity. More specifically, my mission is to heal the world; make it a better place; and play, enjoy, have fun, and rest.

I would like loving each other and living in good-feeling states to be the norm, where we enjoy ourselves most of the time. After all, we spend our lives together yet in different communities, so if you don't enjoy your own company, why would anyone else?

This book provides instructional material on how to raise your frequency as well as instant downloads that enter your energy field directly as you read them—if you agree to get them. They are downloads that have been channeled through me from God, nature, and source, whatever you may call the higher power directing the show.

I was in an induced coma at one point in my life, and after that, I woke up with the idea of the love and light energy field and the happiness experiment. I also had an entirely new understanding of who God is and how much a life of contribution means to me.

Therefore, in the spirit of contribution, I wrote this book to share one of the most powerful energy fields I have discovered, in addition to the powerful tool of transmutation with which to access the field.

This book is different from other books on raising one's vibration because just by reading this, you get your love and light team—or *council,* which will be with you throughout your life—as well as downloads of this powerful high vibration directly into your energy field. This also affects how your energy field interacts with the world. By reading this book, your whole energy and its interaction with the rest of the world will be in a "love and light" manner, creating miracles in your life as well as others' lives just by your having raised your frequency.

It is best to read this book multiple times, making notes of different ideas that jump out each time you read it. It is written in a comprehensive, easy-to-read manner and is meant to change your attitude toward life, making your whole existence a pleasurable experience.

ACKNOWLEDGMENTS

I would like to acknowledge and thank my loving parents, who have supported me throughout my life; my great friends, who have been with me up until now; Balboa Press for holding my hand throughout writing this book; and the whole of humanity and planet Earth, without which this book and my mission wouldn't exist.

CHAPTER 1

THE ORIGINS OF THE LOVE AND LIGHT FIELD

I HAD A CRAZY PSYCHOTIC meltdown. I was screaming like crazy in the hospital hallways, I was severely agitated. The professionals in that hospital did not know how to deal with my mental breakdown. I was put into an induced coma to be transported to a hospital in another country. I woke up from that still psychotic and thinking, *Why don't I see the light?*

Little did I know what I would discover over the next several months. I had been in a field, which I now call the love and light field, where I downloaded a special ability to manipulate energy in the highest and best way with my mind's eye, or third eye.

A few months later, I was in my bed, depressed. I hadn't gotten out of bed, other than to go to the bathroom or to eat something, for about a month. Suddenly, on my way to the bathroom, feeling like I was never going to get out of my depression, I remembered that a year earlier, I had been so happy that I thought I would be happy for the rest of my life. Therefore, I realized that this burden of blackness, fear, and depression that felt everlasting would someday pass too.

However, that led me to question what the purpose of life is. I realized that the only time I felt I had a purpose was when I was happy. So the purpose must be happiness!

I went back to bed and again remembered the time when I was so happy and thought I had all the answers. I had lived by the secret; I had come up with the methods to be happy my entire life. Some of them are what I discuss in this book:

- Meditation
- Exercise
- Gratitude journal
- Yoga

In addition, I began drinking water with lemon, eating healthy food, asking the right questions, and learning every day.

As I was lying there completely depleted of energy, in the miserable black hole of depression, having fear and anxiety attacks around twenty times a day, I was thinking, ironically, *This is great. I know how to write a book on how to live a great life. The question is how on earth am I going to get myself to do it?* I was still unable to move out of bed for longer distances than to go to the bathroom and back. I was broken and almost in a vegetative state. However, I also had an epiphany!

I knew the power of strong intention. I also had a faith crisis during this period, so I wasn't sure God existed. I prayed anyway. As a backup, I addressed evolved aliens as well. I figured that since we humans exist, others who are smarter and have more answers must exist too. It went like this:

Dear God or evolved aliens, please figure out a way for me to be happy without my having to lift a finger or do anything about it. Just make me happy.

I set the intent to be happy. Sure enough, that intent was heard, and within one year, I was traveling to different retreats and personal development courses all over the world. It didn't feel hard; I was doing what I loved. I would get up to write. I would feel bursts of energy to write about the happiness experiment, which is basically an experiment run by God or evolved aliens to promote happiness in people.

The way that originated was that months before the psychotic breakdown, when I was taking a shower during a particularly difficult time of my life, I felt a power grabbing me. I heard clearly, with my clairaudience, "This is an experiment. We don't know the result."

I spent a few days wondering about what had happened, and then I went to an energy worker I had booked previously, when I was going through a particularly stressful time. Within minutes, she said, "I have to tell you something. I have a clear message for you: 'You are in an experiment; we don't know the result.'"

I was shocked, especially because she had used the exact words I had heard in the shower a few days earlier. I asked her for details. She couldn't give me any. She said that the only answers she was getting was that this was an experiment I had signed up for before this lifetime, for the course of several lifetimes, with souls from different planets, and that it had to do with evolution.

During my epiphany that the purpose of life is to be happy, I had known about this experiment. I decided that if that was possible, which was the only explanation

I had found for the unexplainable events and experiences in my life, I could also change it. I wasn't sure that I was a part of any experiment; I was skeptical. But I knew that evolved beings did experiments, so if they did evolution experiments, why not a happiness experiment too!

I used all my willpower to create myself as a part of the happiness experiment instead of whatever fucked-up experiment I had been a part of. I decided that if aliens did experiments and the purpose of the universe is expansion, surely someone out there—be it God, be it another conscious species—would create and conduct the happiness experiment.

This is the first time I accessed what I call the love and light field. I went into the energy world of this lifetime of mine, combined with the origins of this so-called evolution experiment, and I erased it and added the happiness experiment. I had just done my first significant energy work. During this psychotic time, the happiness experiment was born.

While I was depressed, I would also see a lot of darkness around me. When I heard voices that told me they would kill me and that they were following me, I did what I had learned. I didn't know who these voices I hallucinated belonged to—whether they were demons, negative aliens, or negative people—but what I knew was energy work. So I did what I knew.

In the darkness, I was seeing with my clairvoyance, I would add light to the voices telling me they would kill me and were following me. I added light in everything in my life, including myself. At one point, I imagined the origin of my life and everything in it and added light while having the intent to transmute it.

In that session, I also imagined the origin of all that *is*—everything in the omniverse—and I added light. I spent my days working with energy and adding light everywhere and anywhere I could get access to. I also read the book *Love Yourself Like Your Life Depends on It*, by Kamal Ravikant, and I would repeat the mantra *I love myself* all the time. I also read the book *Ho'oponopono* and repeated four statements—I love you, I thank you, please forgive me, and I am sorry—to my demons and death threats.

During the fearful times, I had big questions such as "What is all that is?" One time I felt an energy grab me and heard a voice say, "The omniverse." I knew it was all that is. I was terrified, but I knew I had to figure out a way to work with it. Eventually, I came up with the "I allow the omniverse" method, inspired by ThetaHealing.

In the following months, as I was feeling better, I came up with different theories of who God is. One of them was that God is the benevolent being or consciousness or energy directing the flow of the omniverse in the highest and best way for all involved. Another one was that God is all there is and is the collection of everything in the omniverse in a complete oneness. Another one was that God is the coherent energy bonding all of us as it is within all.

I slowly became familiar with the love and light field, which seemed to have all the answers. I thought, *Well, happiness is not the only purpose of life; living in the love and light field is.* This is how the love and light field idea originated.

Follow me, sending light through me to those voices. Follow me, saying "I am sorry; please forgive me. Thank you. I love you." Following me, saying "I love myself."

Eventually, those voices became good. Those previous demons who were saying they would kill me and were following me started telling me that I look good and I am smart, praising me in all sorts of ways. That is how I knew the power of love and light.

CHAPTER 2

WHAT IS THE LOVE AND LIGHT FIELD?

THE LOVE AND LIGHT FIELD is a segment of consciousness designed to facilitate good energy work and a good life. It is an infinite field close to source consciousness. It is most commonly imagined with white, pink, gold, blue, or green energy. Anywhere there is darkness, you can imagine plugging these colors in and lighting it up, grounding whatever was dark in the light or color of choice. It is a field that has six known definitions.

The first one facilitates longevity of a current good lifetime. If this lifetime does not feel good, this field introduces those good feelings and good events, situations, and context. Longevity refers either to an actual long life or a long enough life to fulfill the life purpose—basically, the perfect amount of time in your current incarnation.

The second definition of the love and light field is also the space of feelings and states of that which is based on love. These include prosperity, wisdom, joy, happiness, enlightenment, harmony, peace, appreciation, compassion, loving intelligence, gratitude, grace, good social relationships, bliss, optimum health, well-being, optimum amounts of all that is good in life, and so forth.

On top of that, it includes everything needed—such as consciousness, awareness, and wisdom—for each to create his or her own love and light. All of these qualities are to be expressed when at its highest and best.

For example, to solve a physics equation, what is needed is intelligence, perseverence, and determination in the highest and best order, in addition to quantity and quality. Based on love, what qualities would you add? Being capable? Being good enough? Being a champion? It is a field that keeps expanding as good-feeling states, feelings, and situations pop up. Also, it provides the good context to have these blissful feelings more often, enables good experiences to come into your life, and facilitates bad situations to become good.

This field has no opposites. It is just one field where

everything is good, serving us and for us. It is a love that holds no opposites, so around 25 percent of the love and light field is reserved for our shadows, feelings of fear, guilt, shame, and terror. Why? To make peace with them or to ascend them or to know how to work with them for good and loving results. If you feel any of these lower frequencies and you started working with the love and light field, simply ask, "What are you here to tell me?"

I once got an impulse that I had to go to the spa. Upon my arrival, I overheard my happiness coach talking shit about me, and I was super stressed and shaking. I don't normally shake when bad things happen. Somehow, the love and light field took me to the spa to see he was a bad coach and then ignited in me the TRE (trauma release exercise) method of shaking the anxiety and stress away. Of course, as soon as I got home, I sent him an email saying I quit his coaching. The field knew how to tell me the truth, took me there, and knew how to instantly release the anxiety and the fear about my coaching not being confidential.

This leads to the third definition, which is that it facilitates good energy work. Tapping into and working with the love and light energy field guarantees these blissful results that create a pronoic life and state of mind. *Pronoia* is the opposite of *paranoia*. It essentially means living life based on the assumption that the omniverse and universe—as well as God, source, and Creator—have your back.

Even if something goes wrong, it will work itself out for the better and allow you to live in bliss. This does not mean you will not be tempted to feel jealous, angry, afraid, or sad—it means you will go through these states with the assumption that it works itself out and know deep down that everything is okay. This does not mean that you never have to lift a finger or take the right action. It means that more often than not, the right action just flows and, as a consequence, so does the right result.

The fourth definition is bringing your light side into peace with your shadow side until you become fully light. The light side is basically all of these easy-to-feel, pleasurable states of existence, and the shadow side is the one you used to run from. These, such as being sad or terrified, are perfectly normal states of consciousness, and the love and light field includes them with the nuance of peace and being okay with them. They are not the opposite of these blissful states; they are complementary to them. Once you reach the ability to be afraid while knowing it is all good in essence, or to feel sad with the underlying presence of peace taking over, you might find yourself fully light or enlightened.

This can also be thought of as the love that has no opposites. Peter Deunov described it this way: "There are three kinds of love, human love, spiritual love, and divine love. Human love varies and changes. Spiritual love never changes but varies. Divine love never changes, never varies."

The shadow of being terrified, for example, has the light side of being in the flow of peace. However, in this definition, being your light side, in peace with your shadow side until you become fully light, refers to the type of light side that has no opposite, just as Peter Deunov described the divine love, a love that has no opposite—a light that is fully you, unconditionally. You get to the point of experiencing all of life in this light and love without opposition or condition, which is fully there regardless of your thoughts, actions, decisions, just being your radiating light and love side in a way that never varies, never changes. It is pure divine love and light, with zero opposites. As Dr. Wayne Dyer said, it is a love that has no opposites, a joy that has no opposites, a state of all inclusivity with an underlining essence of pronoia, of being in peace with it all, and knowing how fully supported you are. That is you becoming your light side.

The fifth aspect of the love and light field is raising the consciousness of the species you are in and the planet you are on—in our case, the human species and planet Earth. If you are a human vibrating at enlightenment resonating at seven-hundred-plus hertz per second, you might raise the consciousness of humanity to resonate even higher, over seven thousand hertz per second, the vibration of an enlightened archangel.

This is a seed of intent, achievable over the next ten to one thousand generations to come. The idea is to raise the vibration of humanity as well and as high as possible to be even with that of an archangel. This happens automatically in the love and light field if you are willing and able. Most likely, you are able if you are willing, as it includes capability. The vibration of the planet is also rising the more we have and do loving and light intents, questions, rituals, blessings, and groundings of the love and light energy field into the earth.

The last known definition, the sixth, is raising your awareness, consciousness, and level of insight and wisdom as high as possible about yourself, your desires, fears, authenticity, and the role you play in the world around you.

Which of the loving and light field definitions do you tap into? Do you have any inspirations, insights, or ideas of what it could be? Are you tuned in yet? If you are willing, tuning into this field happens automatically as you read this book. Are you willing? Is this the best energy field that you have come across?

I know it is my favorite of any field I have ever encountered, and the best part of it is that it is ever expanding, meaning that any ideas you might have that are different from what is here, based on love, might well be part of the love and light field.

To conclude, the less enjoyable parts of love and light and living lovingly and lightly according to the field are 25 percent fear-based stuff, making peace with your shadow, and raising your awareness. The 25 percent of fear-based stuff and emotions such as guilt, anger, sadness, and terror are often part of your shadow side. It is important to learn how to manage them, how to ascend them, or how to make peace with them. The part about raising your awareness is what teaches you to listen to even those so-called bad emotions and change direction if they indicate so. For example, if normally you are an outgoing person but you feel terrified of leaving home today, it could mean it is best to cancel your plans and stay home. Who knows? Maybe you dodged a bullet and avoided an accident.

Sometimes when you increase your awareness, your whole consciousness might receive a shock and you might have a distorted image of reality for a while until you can make some meaning out of what you see and grow aware of. If you were a complete God believer and thought there was one and only one true God and then you grew aware that in the world there might be more deities, you might be shocked. Sometimes growing your awareness creates different shocks in you, and on the positive side, there might be surprises.

CHAPTER 3

THE LOVE AND LIGHT TEAM

THE LOVE AND LIGHT TEAM is an essential part of living a loving and light life. It is an energetic team for your support and is formed of energies, aliens, people, angels, archangels, and God. It is comprised of plenty of groups looking out for your best interests and including your living love and light life into their mission. They include, but are not limited to, the following:

1. The love and light connection team connects and organizes all loving and light teams. This is essential to all the love and light teams working together in harmony and all of them getting to voice their opinions. This is the one you are encouraged to talk with the most. It knows all the

teams and can give you a heads-up if one of the teams has something important to say. You know how some people ask, "Have you talked to your guides about it?" Well, I ask, "Have you talked to your connection team about it?"

2. The love and light reconnection team reconnects you to the loving and light energy of the omniverse. The book *The reconnection* by Eric Pearl talks about the reconnective healing frequencies that return you to "an optimal state of balance that results from interacting with its fully comprehensive spectrum of frequencies consisting of energy, light, and information."

This is an energy you'd want to connect with, right? Luckily for you, there is a whole team designed to do just that—and more. Eric Pearl wrote, "Recent studies have even shown that this spectrum brings about a distinctly beneficial transformation in our DNA. ... It restores coherence and harmony in our lives and transforms our bodies, hearts, minds, and souls physically, mentally, emotionally, spiritually, and in many ways that otherwise may seem impossible." The reconnective force we are talking about includes the healing one and connects you to the loving intelligence and unconditional love of the omniverse and safety on a much higher level by reconnecting you straight to the love and light origins of this omniverse.

3. The loving and light blessing team blesses you with loving and light energies. Christie Marie Sheldon said that when she calibrated herself by giving someone a blessing and by saying "I bless you," it measured at 625, and when she said, "I bless you with pure love and light. I bless you with pure source energy," it measured at 760. Imagine having a team that keeps blessing you, your thoughts, your actions, your feelings, your decisions, your friends, your family, and your life with pure love and light and pure source energy all day, all night, all the time. Wouldn't that be wonderful! Well, that is what the love and light blessing team is for. Therefore, as you would imagine, this team raises your frequency enormously.

4. The loving and light question and intent team asks loving and light questions and sets loving

and light intentions and declarations. As we have already covered, questions and intents are highly important. In fact, I would say they are most important. Imagine a whole team surrounding your energy field all the time with questions such as "Can [your name] be happy?", "Can [your name] be well?", "Can [your name] be fulfilled?" On top of that are intents and declarations such as "May she/he/they be happy," "May she/he/they be well," and "May he/she/ they be fulfilled." These questions, intentions, and declarations go straight into your energy field and raise your frequency.

5. The loving and light archangel team and safety team ensures your integral (psychological, emotional, mental, physical, etheric, spiritual, and energetic) safety. They have methods such as the redirection bubble, which surrounds you and ensures that only the most loving light energies get into your vibrational field and redirect all other energies to where they would be loving and light. Or the transformation spell transforms lower frequencies into loving and light ones.

Also, the transmutation sword can cut through you, your connections, your aura, your consciousness, and your cords to ensure that only the most loving and light energies are attached to you and surround you and that you vibrate at the most loving and light frequencies. There is also the love bomb that they detonate around you in emergencies to ensure that your vibration is one of love and everything interacting with you is as well.

6. The loving and light medical team ensures your health and healthy lifestyle. This particular group includes evolved beings who treat you and your health with various medicines or give you insights as to medicines you should take or doctors you should consult. There are so many remedies that humans have simply not discovered yet, so this team is formed mostly of beings who are here to assist from different planets. Rest assured that the remedies they use have a success rate of health, 80 percent or higher, and this has been proven over the course of more than twenty years. These benevolent beings are here to give you the gift of other planetary science, with your permission, of course.

7. The loving and light prayer team says loving and light prayers. This group prays for a living. Literally. Their prayers are omniversal loving and light ones that invoke the ascended masters, the archangels, and God himself/herself to introduce powerful prayer programs and fields in your aura.

8. The loving and light God team ensures good godly connection. The God team is special in the sense that it ensures connection to the Prime Creator. It also ensures connection to the benevolent being of the omniverse and guarantees that you are in touch with source.

   On top of that, it connects you to the divine energy within each as you are in contact. As you speak with others, the God team ensures that you speak from your godly aspect to theirs, ensuring smooth conversations. This godly team also lets you channel God/source/intelligence and speak straight from the highest wisdom of the omniverse.

9. The loving and light intuition team gives insight to the loving and light team about you, including a body scan. This team is there to enhance your

connection to your own highest self as well as to the highest self of the omniverse. They also scan your bodies—your physical one, your mental one, your emotional one, your psychological one, and your etheric one (also known as your aura and your energy centers)—each day to ensure you are well. If you are not well, they advise the appropriate team to rectify that so you feel and are your best self. They remove blocks and notify the connection team of what to do next.

10. The loving and light therapy team ensures confidential private therapy for you. This happens often throughout the day; within your thoughts, they interact with you and release you from your worries, fears, grief, sadness, and so forth. You get glimpses of conversations, ideas, and insights and respond almost automatically, without having to put in any effort, and your most loving and light life is ensured. This personal therapy is mostly telepathy at its best.

11. The loving and light privacy team ensures your privacy when needed. This team seems to know to put you in touch with the right places, things, or people that are there for you, without having

to worry about anything such as the smallest gossip about you spreading or the most intimate conversation you had going public.

12. The loving and light confidentiality team keeps confidentiality of the loving and light team's workings. Basically, all the loving and light team does in relation to you is strictly confidential, only for you, them, and God. It is up to you what you share.

13. The loving and light translator team translates different messages across the connection team. This is an essential team given that different races and forms of beings and angels and archangels work together in your energy team. The translation team is there to make sure everyone is understood and heard.

14. The loving and light traveler team ensures you are in a loving and light environment. This team gives you insights of where to go or be in order for you to be in the most loving and light place. It goes to the extent of almost teleporting you to a different reality field or dimension if you really are in the wrong place at the wrong time.

15. The loving and light transmutation team of you and your environment transmutes both you and your environment to ensure that you are of the highest and best love and light vibrations and surrounded by those as well. Here again, the transmutation sword comes into play as do other tools, such as the transmutation powder that they throw around you to make sure the area you are in is transmuted;whatever tools you can imagine for the purpose of transmutation, they probably have them.

16. The loving and light relationship team ensures loving and light relationships. This team understands the value of relationships. The longest study ever is the ongoing Harvard study of adult development, and it started in 1938, during the Great Depression. The results show that the people who lean on those around them for support and have people to lean on are the happiest, healthiest individuals. It also shows that the quality, not quantity, of relationships is the most important. The relationship team focuses on putting you in touch with the most qualitative people for you and ensures a good-quality relationship with

them. The relationship team is essentially a social advantage for you.

17. The loving and light hiring team hires loving and light energies (people, aliens, archangels, and other beings). This hiring team decides who would be a good match for you and hires them to be on your team. They make sure that the beings working for you respect your beliefs and principals and get the best match for you.

18. The loving and light workplace team ensures that you have a loving and light workplace. This team ensures that your loving and light team has a nice celebratory and happy workplace for them to be able to do their best work on you by creating different challenges, prizes, and praises for each loving and light team each day. And of course it also ensures that you have the best workplace by moving you toward a company you would prefer working for or putting you in touch with the right people for your best job opportunities.

19. The loving and light play team plays to ensure loving and light results and processes for you. Basically, this is a team that plays with you for a living. They give you different ideas of games you

can play in your head or fun and healthy activities through which you manifest the energy of joy.

20. This loving and light team adds teams according to your other needs and wants. This team adds different groups to ensure you are living your most loving and light life according to your needs and preferences.

21. The loving and light accelerating learning team ensures you are learning that which guarantees you loving and light processes and results. They essentially have you participating actively in different activities that will lead you to a great journey and results, whatever that may be for you.

This is a list of teams I found valuable. Which one is your favorite? What would you add? Please let me know on Facebook: Ana Lior or the Love and Light Field Facebook page.

CHAPTER 4

HELPING YOUR LOVING AND LIGHT TEAM

ONCE YOU HAVE ACCEPTED HAVING a loving and light team, you have one. They can work by themselves without any help from you, but they are most efficient if you help them. Here are ways in which you can help your loving and light team.

The loving and light connection team can be helped by interacting with them, similar to how you would talk to your guides. You can ask them what their plan for today is or how you can assist them. You can also ask them questions that they then answer by combining what the other teams know: "What do you think about my aiming to manifest $1 million? Is it too high a goal? Too low? Is it achievable?"

"What do you think about Marie? Is she a good

friend? A bad one? Is she someone I would like to get close to? Or should I stay far away from her?" You can address literally any question you have to the connection team. Have you talked to your connection team about it?

On top of that, you can debrief them and have them debrief the rest of the teams daily, weekly, monthly, or even just yearly. Ask them four questions I learned in a business course about how to improve services and how to increase sales. Only in this case, it would be how to improve your life and increase interaction with the love and light field.

The first question of debriefing is "What did you learn?" Therefore, you would ask your love and light connection team, "What did you learn today/ this week/ this month/ this year?" You may or may not hear an answer. It depends how intuitive you are. They would then ask every other team the same. Ultimately, you could ask yourself, "What did I learn?"

The second question is "What worked well out of the things we did today?"

The third one is "What didn't work well?"

The fourth is "What would you improve?"

You can also help the connection team by expressing your preferences and priorities, saying things such as

"I would like to weigh one hundred and twenty-five pounds," "I would like to be in great shape," "I would like to earn ten thousand or more dollars per month," and "I would like to be fulfilled." The popular belief in the law of attraction is that you have to think of your manifestations as already manifested. So say, "I weigh one hundred and twenty-five pounds." Saying "I would like to" or "I want to" expresses to the universe that you don't have it yet. That is partially true.

However, in order to manifest something, in some cases, you also have to acknowledge where you are now. Just in case the previous is true, this connection team space is a safe space where you can express your frustrations and preferences without sending the wrong message to the universe.

You can help the loving and light reconnection team by creating a reconnection ritual. From time to time, you move around freely in a way that feels good to you, and you ground in light, imagining light from above coming through you, out to your hands, into your aura, and out your feet, into the center of the earth, and then coming back to you from the center, through you, out your hands again, into your aura, and into space outside your head. Do this until your aura is filled up as you move around and then feel free to enjoy the rest of your day. This also helps balance the earth energy as you fill it with fresh light from the cosmos and you exchange old energy from the earth.

You can assist the love and light blessing team by again being filled with light from the cosmos and the earth, letting it compose your aura, and feeling the blessing energy, all the while saying "I bless me with pure love and light. I bless me with the highest and best omniversal energy. I bless us with pure love and light. I bless us with the highest and best omniversal energy." (This can refer to anyone or anything.) You can do this as often as you would like. Doing it raises your energy, and the more you get into the habit of doing it, the better you will feel.

The loving and light questions and intent team can be assisted by asking the right questions. As covered in the intent chapter, a right question would lead you to the desired outcome. Great questions you could have in your inner dialogue would be *How can I raise my happiness? How can I raise my income? How can I be safe? How can health, wealth, and wisdom flow through me and to me? How can I be in the most loving and light vibrational patterns and flow?* Intentions and declarations are also valuable, as we have seen. *I am healthy, wealthy, and wise. I am well. I am prosperous. I am amazing. I am awesome. I am in flow. Miracles happen everyday and everyday they come my way.*

The loving and light archangel team and safety team can be helped by imagining yourself inside a bubble that allows only what is loving and light to enter, keeps what is loving and light when it is so, and sends the rest out to when and where it could be loving and light. Also imagine a wand with which you instantly transform non-loving and light frequencies. On top of it is an imaginary sword with which you cut through the cords attached to you, ensuring they are transmuted, or even through you, ensuring that your energies are transmuted. Along with the transmutation fire, this is the more aggressive method to ensure that only that which is loving and light stays in your energy field.

The transmutation fire is a white bonfire that you place in you and around you to get rid of any lower energies or negative ones. You can also imagine a pink bomb filled with love that you throw in heavy, dense energy situations and make them light energies. You can use these techniques as often as you would like, whenever and wherever you are.

The loving and light medical team can be helped by your going to the doctor for regular checkups and by going to different holistic healers.

You can assist the love and light prayer team by praying. A powerful prayer usually begins with "I hereby invoke God, the archangels of love and light, the angels of love and light, and the ascended masters of love and light to help me with …" This can follow with any of your desires—for example, " … to help me find the perfect job." It usually ends with "Dear God, archangels, angels and ascended masters, I thank you."

The loving and light God team can be helped by your imagining a spark in the center of your heart, your divine connection, as often as you would like. Especially whenever you talk to others, you can imagine that spark in your center and in theirs, and when you talk, a light grid forms between you, symbolizing your talking to their divine spark in a divine dialogue.

Your loving and light intuition team can be assisted by daily meditation to increase your intuition. Also, you can give yourself body scans from time to time. Simply close your eyes and start at the top of your head (imagining the energy there), moving down your head to your eyes, your ears, your nose, your cheeks, your mouth, your throat, your shoulders, your arms, your heart, and all the way to the bottom of your feet. If you see any abnormalities or feel any pain, you can invoke the love and light field to correct it—and then you should probably see a doctor about it.

You can also bless your energy centers starting at your root chakra, at the lowest part of your torso, the perineum, or the base of your spine. "I bless you with pure love and light; I bless you with the highest and best omniversal energy."

Then move on to the sacral chakra, two fingers under your navel. "I bless you with pure love and light; I bless you with the highest and best omniversal energy."

Then there is the solar plexus chakra, located in the upper abdomen, just below the rib cage. "I bless you, ... omniversal energy."

Next comes the heart chakra, at the heart. "I bless you, ... omniversal energy."

After that comes the throat chakra. "I bless you,. ... omniversal energy."

The following is the third eye chakra, which again we bless.

We then bless the crown chakra, which is located at the middle of the forehead.

Lastly, we bless our whole aura. "I bless my aura with pure love and light; I bless my aura with the highest and best omniversal energy for me."

We can help our loving and light therapy team by going to therapy or doing therapy on ourselves, asking them to hold space for us and asking ourselves "What bothered me today? Why did it bother me? What fears popped up? Why did I have those fears? What frustrated me? Why did it frustrate me? What's up with me today? How am I?" Or ask any questions a therapist might ask you.

You can help the transmutation team by putting yourself and your environment in a transmutation white or violet fire.

The loving and light relationship team can be helped by your socializing more and better. For example, you can learn the five love languages and pay attention to those you have around you. If someone around you likes gifts, you can make sure you buy him a little something every now and again. If someone likes touch, you can hug her. If someone likes quality time spent together, you can spend more time with him. If someone likes words of affirmation, you can focus on complimenting her. Finally, if someone likes acts of service, you can help him clean the house and reorganize his closet or cook him something from time to time. You generally can tell what people like by what they offer.

You can help the loving and light workplace team by celebrating your victories and choosing to praise your team, telling them thank you, and generally having fun.

The same goes for the play team. You can, for example, also imagine your life as a cartoon or a theater play, and in this way, it would probably be a lot more enjoyable. You can do stuff you liked as a kid—hop around, dance, blow bubbles—anything to manifest the energy of joy into your life.

The loving and light team can be helped by your adding teams in your life according to what you feel you need or prefer. If you prefer having a debriefing team, you can just add it. Or add a gratitude team that gives thanks all day long. The possibilities are infinite.

CHAPTER 5

INTENT

THE POWER OF INTENT IS covered in this book. One of the beginning phases of my feeling as if life is worthwhile was the intent to be happy. Intent can be expressed in several ways, one of which is simply "I would like to be happy." Another powerful way is writing on a piece of paper "My intent is to be in a flow of joy by January 2021." This is more powerful because you have a deadline.

What is even more powerful than that is to be able to measure it somehow. What would your life look like if you were in a state of joy? In this context, an example of what you could write is "I would like to live by the beach, in a villa, enjoying beautiful sunsets and sunrises, having a direct view of the sea/ocean, and thinking multiple times a day how grateful I am and truly meaning it with every fiber of my being. I would like to laugh with friends at least once a week and feel how loved I truly am with every cell, all by January 2021."

"What is even more powerful than this?" you might be asking. It's just that—*asking*. An example would be "How can I be in the flow of joy by 2021? How can I be in a state of gratitude by thinking several times a day how grateful I am and meaning it? How can I enjoy seeing the beach every morning when I wake up? How can I laugh with my friends? How can I have fun more often?"

Christie Marie Sheldon has a powerful method to manifest. It's called "What would it take?" She manifests for herself and tens of thousands of clients by asking the universe the question of "What would it take to …?" In this context, What would it take for me to live in a flow of joy? What would it take for me to be truly grateful for my life several times a day? What would it take for me to have friends? What would it take for me to laugh with them? What would it take for me to have more fun? Then she adds the intention that anything in the way of it be transmuted across all times, dimensions, spaces, and realities.

I noticed that the most powerful way of materializing

an intent is saying "I allow and encourage the omniverse to ..." This method is inspired by ThetaHealing. The reason this is so powerful is that it uses the universal truth of the law of allowance. As Laura Silva says, there is great power in allowing yourself to be a certain way, such as happy. She says there are two interpretations of this law. One is to allow others to be exactly as they would like and do exactly what they would like. Another one is to allow yourself to have fun, to be joyous. "I allow myself to live in the love and light field" is a statement you could use.

However, playing on the law of allowance, you could allow the whole omniverse to have you live a certain way. Imagine having the whole omniverse conspire with you to meet your desires. The omniverse is benevolent; therefore, surely it would meet your encouragements. The next chapter of this book is filled with downloads from the omniverse, and you can read it over several days.

This also originates from the art of surrender. What if the Omniverve, wanted everything you want for you, and all you need to do is surrender and receive and let it provide. Just like the saying- the universe provides.

CHAPTER 6

I ALLOW AND ENCOURAGE YOU, OMNIVERSE TO...

I ALLOW AND ENCOURAGE YOU, omniverse, to have me be happy.

I allow and encourage you, omniverse, to have me be grateful.

I allow and encourage you, omniverse, to have me be graceful.

I allow and encourage you, omniverse, to have me be well.

I allow and encourage you, omniverse, to have me be joyous.

I allow and encourage you, omniverse, to have me be aligned with love and light.

I allow and encourage you, omniverse, to have me be compassionate.

I allow and encourage you, omniverse, to have me loving.

I allow and encourage you, omniverse, to have me live in the love and light field.

I allow and encourage you, omniverse, to have to me lovingly intelligent.

I allow and encourage you, omniverse, to have me be wise.

I allow and encourage you, omniverse, to have me be highly intelligent.

I allow and encourage you, omniverse, to have me live in alpha brain waves.

I allow and encourage you, omniverse, to have me be safe.

I allow and encourage you, omniverse, to have me have loving connections.

I allow and encourage you, omniverse, to have me have loving relationships.

I allow and encourage you, omniverse, to have me have loving friendships.

I allow and encourage you, omniverse, to have me have safe friendships.

I allow and encourage you, omniverse, to have me have safe relationships.

I allow and encourage you, omniverse, to have me have safe connections.

I allow and encourage you, omniverse, to have me live in a loving flow.

I allow and encourage you, omniverse, to have me live in a safe flow.

I allow and encourage you, omniverse, to have me live in a joyous flow.

I allow and encourage you, omniverse, to have me be caring.

I allow and encourage you, omniverse, to have me be blessed.

I allow and encourage you, omniverse, to have me be successful.

I allow and encourage you, omniverse, to have me thrive.

I allow and encourage you, omniverse, to have me be peaceful.

I allow and encourage you, omniverse, to have me be present.

I allow and encourage you, omniverse, to have me be aware.

I allow and encourage you, omniverse, to have me be conscious.

I allow and encourage you, omniverse, to have me transmuted.

I allow and encourage you, omniverse, to have all my connections transmuted.

I allow and encourage you, omniverse, to have all my relationships transmuted.

I allow and encourage you, omniverse, to have all my friendships transmuted.

I allow and encourage you, omniverse, to have all my existence transmuted.

I allow and encourage you, omniverse, to have all my life transmuted.

I allow and encourage you, omniverse, to have every thought I have transmuted.

I allow and encourage you, omniverse, to have every decision I make be transmuted.

I allow and encourage you, omniverse, to have every incarnation I have be transmuted.

I allow and encourage you, omniverse, to have all my decisions come out of the love and light field.

I allow and encourage you, omniverse, to have the base of my existence be the love and light field.

I allow and encourage you, omniverse, to have the base of my life be the love and light field.

I allow and encourage you, omniverse, to have the base of every connection I have be the love and light field.

I allow and encourage you, omniverse, to have every base of every thought I have be the love and light field.

I allow and encourage you, omniverse, to have me laugh often.

I allow and encourage you, omniverse, to have me make the best decisions.

I allow and encourage you, omniverse, to have me transcend lower frequencies.

I allow and encourage you, omniverse, to have me live in higher frequencies.

I allow and encourage you, omniverse, to have me be charismatic.

I allow and encourage you, omniverse, to have me be a magnet of love and light.

I allow and encourage you, omniverse, to have me be inspired.

I allow and encourage you, omniverse, to have me channel the love and light field.

I allow and encourage you, omniverse, to have me express the love and light field.

I allow and encourage you, omniverse, to have me live the love and light field.

I allow and encourage you, omniverse, to have me be strong.

I allow and encourage you, omniverse, to have me be resilient.

I allow and encourage you, omniverse, to have me live life with only fun challenges.

I allow and encourage you, omniverse, to have me enjoy life.

I allow and encourage you, omniverse, to have me laugh through life.

I allow and encourage you, omniverse, to have me be great with myself.

I allow and encourage you, omniverse, to have me be great with people.

I allow and encourage you, omniverse, to have me be healthy.

I allow and encourage you, omniverse, to have me do the loving and light practices.

I allow and encourage you, omniverse, to have me do that which is loving and light daily.

I allow and encourage you, omniverse, to have me live by that which is loving and light.

I allow and encourage you, omniverse, to have me eat healthy.

I allow and encourage you, omniverse, to have all my environment transmuted.

I allow and encourage you, omniverse, to have all I ingest and inhale and touch be transmuted.

I allow and encourage you, omniverse, to have all of my ways of being transmuted.

I allow and encourage you, omniverse, to have every atom of my being transmuted.

I allow and encourage you, omniverse, to have every atom of my environment transmuted.

I allow and encourage you, omniverse, to have every cell of my being transmuted.

I allow and encourage you, omniverse, to have every cell of my environment transmuted.

I allow and encourage you, omniverse, to have the space between the spaces transmuted.

I allow and encourage you, omniverse, to have the space before the thoughts transmuted.

I allow and encourage you, omniverse, to have the perfect home for me delivered to me under my name.

I allow and encourage you, omniverse, to provide me with all the money I could ever wish for.

I allow and encourage you, omniverse, to provide me with the perfect family.

I allow and encourage you, omniverse, to provide me with the best friendships.

I allow and encourage you, omniverse, to provide me with the best car or traveling modality.

I allow and encourage you, omniverse, to have me live in the best city.

I allow and encourage you, omniverse, to have me be surrounded by family and friends.

I allow and encourage you, omniverse, to have the best loving and light team.

I allow and encourage you, omniverse, to have me be fulfilled.

I allow and encourage you, omniverse, to have me be peaceful.

I allow and encourage you, omniverse, to have me be in the best flow.

I allow and encourage you, omniverse, to have me explore my area.

I allow and encourage you, omniverse, to have my sex life be amazing.

I allow and encourage you, omniverse, to have me enjoy every moment of my life.

I allow and encourage you, omniverse, to have me live passionately.

I allow and encourage you, omniverse, to have my relationships with my parents be safe and loving.

I allow and encourage you, omniverse, to have me have the perfect boyfriend/girlfriend.

I allow and encourage you, omniverse, to have me be the perfect lover/boyfriend/girlfriend/husband/ wife

I allow and encourage you, omniverse, to have me have fun often.

I allow and encourage you, omniverse, to have me be in a loving flow.

I allow and encourage you, omniverse, to have me have the perfect companion in life.

I allow and encourage you, omniverse, to have me feel unconditional love.

I allow and encourage you, omniverse, to have me channel superior love and intelligence.

I allow and encourage you, omniverse, to have me be in a flow of love.

I allow and encourage you, omniverse, to calm me.

I allow and encourage you, omniverse, to support me.

I allow and encourage you, omniverse, to direct my energy lovingly and lightly.

I allow and encourage you, omniverse, to feed into my system love and light.

I allow and encourage you, omniverse, to energize me.

I allow and encourage you, omniverse, to have me be free.

I allow and encourage you, omniverse, to have me balanced in the best vibes.

I allow and encourage you, omniverse, to have me be grounded to the love and light of earth.

I allow and encourage you, omniverse, to have me grounded to the love and light of the omniverse.

I allow and encourage you, omniverse, to have me grounded to the love and light of my home.

I allow and encourage you, omniverse, to have me be rich.

I allow and encourage you, omniverse, to have me believe in myself.

I allow and encourage you, omniverse, to have me be motivated.

I allow and encourage you, omniverse, to have me take inspired action.

I allow and encourage you, omniverse, to have me be powerful.

I allow and encourage you, omniverse, to have me stand in my power.

I allow and encourage you, omniverse, to have me be persistent.

I allow and encourage you, omniverse, to have me be relaxed.

I allow and encourage you, omniverse, to have me be 100 percent me.

I allow and encourage you, omniverse, to have me be connected lovingly to all that is.

I allow and encourage you, omniverse, to have me be in the moment.

I allow and encourage you, omniverse, to have me achieve.

I allow and encourage you, omniverse, to have me take bold steps.

I allow and encourage you, omniverse, to have me be a good leader.

I allow and encourage you, omniverse, to have me be driven safely and in the right direction.

I allow and encourage you, omniverse, to have me be valuable.

I allow and encourage you, omniverse, to have me be prosperous.

I allow and encourage you, omniverse, to have me be the master of my own thoughts.

I allow and encourage you, omniverse, to have me be courageous.

I allow and encourage you, omniverse, to have me be a millionaire.

I allow and encourage you, omniverse, to have me have million-dollar ideas.

I allow and encourage you, omniverse, to have me act on my million-dollar ideas.

I allow and encourage you, omniverse, to have me be optimistic.

I allow and encourage you, omniverse, to have me be confident.

I allow and encourage you, omniverse, to have me be healthy.

I allow and encourage you, omniverse, to have me be wealthy.

I allow and encourage you, omniverse, to have me be open to receiving good stuff.

I allow and encourage you, omniverse, to have me be dedicated to good causes.

I allow and encourage you, omniverse, to have me take inspired action today.

I allow and encourage you, omniverse, to have me be persistent.

I allow and encourage you, omniverse, to have me say yes to life.

I allow and encourage you, omniverse, to have me feel oneness.

I allow and encourage you, omniverse, to have me love my life.

I allow and encourage you, omniverse, to have me move forward with confidence.

I allow and encourage you, omniverse, to have me be at home in my own body.

I allow and encourage you, omniverse, to have me be energetic.

I allow and encourage you, omniverse, to have me feel energetic.

I allow and encourage you, omniverse, to have me be disciplined.

I allow and encourage you, omniverse, to have me be enough.

I allow and encourage you, omniverse, to have me be the master of my own emotions.

I allow and encourage you, omniverse, to have me be a billionaire.

I allow and encourage you, omniverse, to have me be expansive in the right ways.

I allow and encourage you, omniverse, to have me be positive.

I allow and encourage you, omniverse, to have me be happy with who I am.

I allow and encourage you, omniverse, to have me be hopeful.

I allow and encourage you, omniverse, to have me be optimistic.

I allow and encourage you, omniverse, to have me be in my power.

I allow and encourage you, omniverse, to have me express myself well.

I allow and encourage you, omniverse, to have me be loved for who I am.

I allow and encourage you, omniverse, to have me be respected for who I am.

I allow and encourage you, omniverse, to have me be honored for who I am.

I allow and encourage you, omniverse, to have me honor life.

I allow and encourage you, omniverse, to have me respect life.

I allow and encourage you, omniverse, to have me love life.

I allow and encourage you, omniverse, to have me love myself.

I allow and encourage you, omniverse, to have me be in command of my life.

I allow and encourage you, omniverse, to have me love my life.

I allow and encourage you, omniverse, to have me live a great life.

I allow and encourage you, omniverse, to have me respect my life.

I allow and encourage you, omniverse, to have me honor my life.

I allow and encourage you, omniverse, to praise me.

I allow and encourage you, omniverse, to have me praise me.

I allow and encourage you, omniverse, to have me appreciate myself for who I am.

I allow and encourage you, omniverse, to have me appreciate my talents.

I allow and encourage you, omniverse, to have me be smart.

I allow and encourage you, omniverse, to transform my best dreams into reality.

I allow and encourage you, omniverse, to have me be comfortable in my skin.

I allow and encourage you, omniverse, to have me look fabulous.

I allow and encourage you, omniverse, to have me know how fabulous I am.

I allow and encourage you, omniverse, to have me power through all my life's situations with a smile.

I allow and encourage you, omniverse, to have me appreciate the confidence that I have.

I allow and encourage you, omniverse, to appreciate me.

I allow and encourage you, omniverse, to accept me.

I allow and encourage you, omniverse, to have me accept me.

I allow and encourage you, omniverse, to have me surround myself with people who inspire me.

I allow and encourage you, omniverse, to have me surround myself with people who accept me.

I allow and encourage you, omniverse, to have me surround myself with people who love me.

I allow and encourage you, omniverse, to have me surround myself with people who respect me.

I allow and encourage you, omniverse, to have me surround myself with people who admire me.

I allow and encourage you, omniverse, to have me surround myself with people I admire.

I allow and encourage you, omniverse, to have me admire myself.

I allow and encourage you, omniverse, to have me know that every situation works out for my highest good.

I allow and encourage you, omniverse, to have me accept feedback well.

I allow and encourage you, omniverse, to have me grow lovingly and lightly.

I allow and encourage you, omniverse, to have me be assertive.

I allow and encourage you, omniverse, to have me speak with authority.

I allow and encourage you, omniverse, to have me believe that everything works out for the best.

I allow and encourage you, omniverse, to prove to me that everything works out for the best.

I allow and encourage you, omniverse, to have me be an amazing leader.

I allow and encourage you, omniverse, to have me embody my highest self.

I allow and encourage you, omniverse, to have me be happy in my own skin.

I allow and encourage you, omniverse, to have me be happy in my circumstances.

I allow and encourage you, omniverse, to have me have a wonderful business in a wonderful way.

I allow and encourage you, omniverse, to have me pay my bills with gratitude.

I allow and encourage you, omniverse, to have me make more than enough money to pay my bills with gratitude.

I allow and encourage you, omniverse, to have me appreciate my body.

I allow and encourage you, omniverse, to have me be happy for the little things.

I allow and encourage you, omniverse, to have me celebrate my success every single day.

I allow and encourage you, omniverse, to celebrate my success with me.

I allow and encourage you, omniverse, to have me be and feel beautiful.

I allow and encourage you, omniverse, to have me be worthy and feel so.

I allow and encourage you, omniverse, to have me help others when they need it.

I allow and encourage you, omniverse, to have me be okay with everything I have done.

I allow and encourage you, omniverse, to have me learn from everything I have done.

I allow and encourage you, omniverse, to have me be the best.

I allow and encourage you, omniverse, to have me see the best in people.

I allow and encourage you, omniverse, to have me be gentle with myself.

I allow and encourage you, omniverse, to have me be willing to change for the better.

I allow and encourage you, omniverse, to have me trust my intuition.

I allow and encourage you, omniverse, to have me trust my path in life.

I allow and encourage you, omniverse, to have me surround myself with people who encourage me.

I allow and encourage you, omniverse, to have me be winning.

I allow and encourage you, omniverse, to have me appreciate everything, especially the good.

I allow and encourage you, omniverse, to have me stand strong.

I allow and encourage you, omniverse, to have me make them wonder how I do it.

I allow and encourage you, omniverse, to have me take time for myself.

I allow and encourage you, omniverse, to have money come to me easily and effortlessly.

I allow and encourage you, omniverse, to have wealth flow into my life.

I allow and encourage you, omniverse, to have me surround myself with people who treat me well.

I allow and encourage you, omniverse, to have me trust my inner wisdom and access it.

I allow and encourage you, omniverse, to have me engage only in work that impacts this world positively.

I allow and encourage you, omniverse, to have me take full responsibility for my results.

I allow and encourage you, omniverse, to have me be centered in love and light.

I allow and encourage you, omniverse, to have people love me and my aura.

I allow and encourage you, omniverse, to have be a money magnet.

I allow and encourage you, omniverse, to have me accept everyone as they are.

I allow and encourage you, omniverse, to have me see the light of this world.

I allow and encourage you, omniverse, to have be a good influencer.

I allow and encourage you, omniverse, to have me be a powerful influencer.

I allow and encourage you, omniverse, to have me be a gift to people.

I allow and encourage you, omniverse, to have people be a gift to me.

I allow and encourage you, omniverse, to have me give wonderful service for wonderful pay.

I allow and encourage you, omniverse, to have me be proud of who I have become.

I allow and encourage you, omniverse, to have me appreciate all that I am.

I allow and encourage you, omniverse, to appreciate all that I am.

I allow and encourage you, omniverse, to love all that I am.

I allow and encourage you, omniverse, to have me be joyous with who I am.

I allow and encourage you, omniverse, to have me be hopeful.

I allow and encourage you, omniverse, to have me be of optimum health.

I allow and encourage you, omniverse, to have me focus.

I allow and encourage you, omniverse, to have my vibration gently tuned to the frequency of source.

I allow and encourage you, omniverse, to have me remember who I am.

I allow and encourage you, omniverse, to have me remember all I need to remember.

I allow and encourage you, omniverse, to have me align with who I truly am.

I allow and encourage you, omniverse, to have me be easy on myself.

I allow and encourage you, omniverse, to have me be nice to myself.

I allow and encourage you, omniverse, to have me enjoy more.

I allow and encourage you, omniverse, to have me be in touch with source.

I allow and encourage you, omniverse, to have me fulfill my purpose.

I allow and encourage you, omniverse, to have me live life better than before.

I allow and encourage you, omniverse, to have me be where I need to be and when.

I allow and encourage you, omniverse, to have me feel the appreciation that source has for me.

I allow and encourage you, omniverse, to have me feel appreciative.

I allow and encourage you, omniverse, to have me understand better that which I need to.

I allow and encourage you, omniverse, to have me learn better.

I allow and encourage you, omniverse, to have my life feel good to me.

I allow and encourage you, omniverse, to wrap me in blessings.

I allow and encourage you, omniverse, to have my life serve me well.

I allow and encourage you, omniverse, to have my best desires materialized in reality.

I allow and encourage you, omniverse, to have my world refresh.

I allow and encourage you, omniverse, to have me find balance every step along the way.

I allow and encourage you, omniverse, to have wonderful things flow to me.

I allow and encourage you, omniverse, to have me flow to wonderful places.

I allow and encourage you, omniverse, to have wonderful people flow to me.

I allow and encourage you, omniverse, to have wonderful situations flow to me.

I allow and encourage you, omniverse, to be lovingly aware of me.

I allow and encourage you, omniverse, to have me satisfy my desires.

I allow and encourage you, omniverse, to have my body be most intelligent.

I allow and encourage you, omniverse, to have my body be well.

I allow and encourage you, omniverse, to have me be at my natural state of maximum well-being.

I allow and encourage you, omniverse, to have me focus on good-feeling thoughts.

I allow and encourage you, omniverse, to have me be guided by source.

I allow and encourage you, omniverse, to have me be guided by the highest omniversal intelligence and love.

I allow and encourage you, omniverse, to have the highest omniversal intelligence and love drive me.

I allow and encourage you, omniverse, to have me listen.

I allow and encourage you, omniverse, to have my physical body heal.

I allow and encourage you, omniverse, to have my emotional body heal.

I allow and encourage you, omniverse, to have my spiritual body heal.

I allow and encourage you, omniverse, to have my etheric body heal.

I allow and encourage you, omniverse, to have my integral body heal.

I allow and encourage you, omniverse, to have my cells improve at every level.

I allow and encourage you, omniverse, to have me tune to my frequency of natural well-being.

I allow and encourage you, omniverse, to have me be inspired by beneficial behavior.

I allow and encourage you, omniverse, to have me practice beneficial behavior.

I allow and encourage you, omniverse, to have me get from where I am to where I desire.

I allow and encourage you, omniverse, to have me be where I desire at all times.

I allow and encourage you, omniverse, to have me experience perfect natural conditions.

I allow and encourage you, omniverse, to have me be aligned with well-being.

I allow and encourage you, omniverse, to have my body benefit.

I allow and encourage you, Omniverse, to have me be forever young or have me age beautifully.

I allow and encourage you, omniverse, to have my life be profitable.

I allow and encourage you, omniverse, to have me be successful in all that I do.

I allow and encourage you, omniverse, to have me be financially abundant.

I allow and encourage you, omniverse, to have me be for the greatest good.

I allow and encourage you, omniverse, to have me be in a space of vitality.

I allow and encourage you, omniverse, to have my abundance become evident.

I allow and encourage you, omniverse, to have me think of money with eagerness and fun.

I allow and encourage you, omniverse, to have me be free of worry and concerns.

I allow and encourage you, omniverse, to have me rediscover my natural state of ease.

I allow and encourage you, omniverse, to have me be happy when others win.

I allow and encourage you, omniverse, to have me be happy when I win.

I allow and encourage you, omniverse, to have me look for beauty.

I allow and encourage you, omniverse, to have me find beauty.

I allow and encourage you, omniverse, to have me be fully present with beauty.

CHAPTER 7

GRATITUDE

GRATITUDE IS ANOTHER GREAT WAY to materialize. It is best to feel the emotion of gratitude each day for both good things that already happened and future things as if they have happened.

What does appreciation and gratefulness mean? Think about it.

Appreciation means increase. An increase of what? Be appreciative of what you would like to increase in your life. Have you ever had a neighbor who played a musical instrument and right when you started to watch a movie, you heard him loudly playing his drums or what have you? What does that feel like? Irritating? Angering?

What is a good response energetically? See if there is anything you can do. What if you think, *Don't play, don't play, don't play.* Will he stop playing? *No.* It is like your kid scratching his knee and you thinking, *Don't bleed*. It's done in vain.

Going back to the question of what are you going to be appreciative of, it should be what you want an increase of in your life. Therefore, in this scenario, you might say, "I am so grateful and thankful that he stopped playing his drums." I am not going to lie—this is not the most powerful method. However, combined with "I allow the omniverse to have my neighbor stop playing drums" and combined with what would it take for the neighbor to stop playing the music, you increase the chance of that happening. However, just being grateful and thankful might make a big difference.

What if he doesn't stop playing? Well, then something shifted already. Now you are grateful and thankful, so you are solution oriented. Next you can be grateful and thankful you have headphones to watch and listen to your movie anyway.

In the other example, of your kid scratching his knee, you can be grateful and thankful for him being calm and more than capable of handling the pain and of you being centered and grounded. Will it happen immediately? *No.* However, the brain learns through repetition. Eventually, you *will* be centered and grounded. Being appreciative of what you would like an increase of is number one.

Then there is gratefulness. I like to think of gratefulness as one of my mentors describes it. What is gratefulness? Think about it. Are you filled with greatness in each moment? The esoteric answer is *Heavens yes, I am a magnificent being filled with greatness in each waking moment and beyond.* Now go tell yourself that in the mirror. I'll wait here.

Have you done it? If so, how does that feel? Great, right? If not, are you thinking, *Yeah, right, as if ...?* In both cases, the reality is that you won't be feeling great in every moment. However, studies show that with the daily practice of gratitude for thirty days, you will increase your *great* feelings by 25 percent. Do you think this increase of happiness is long lasting? It sure is. Studies show that if you partake in the daily practice of gratitude for just thirty days, your increase in happiness of 25 percent increases for the next year and beyond. Appreciate gratefulness. Go to the mirror again and say, "I appreciate gratefulness."

You might ask, "What if there is nothing to be grateful for? What if you have one of those days where you wake up on the wrong side of my bed, your boyfriend breaks up with you, and you lose my job? What a horrible day. Recent studies show that even asking yourself the question "What am I grateful for?" is enough to change the biochemistry in the brain. I learned this from Emily Fletcher.

CHAPTER 8

TRANSMUTATION

ALCHEMISTS DEFINE TRANSMUTATION AS THE supposed alchemical process of changing base metals into gold, such as transforming lead into gold, changing a low-quality material into a high-quality material.

However, what I define as transmutation is slightly different. I will be referring to four definitions I have picked up on from the love and light field that describe transmutation.

My first definition of transmutation is transforming low-energy vibrations into high-energy ones, a.k.a. love and light. It's basically transforming the energy of guilt, shame, or willingness, which carries the vibration of three hundred on the David R. Hawkins scale of consciousness, into one of love, vibrating at five hundred, and the rest of the vibrations the love and light field include, such as enlightenment. As mentioned earlier, the love and light field has an interesting vibration. It can far exceed the vibration of enlightenment for humans, which is measured at one thousand.

The second definition is realigning with love and light. Sometimes it is not necessary to transform something into a higher vibrational pattern; it is sufficient to change directions and go back to the original alignment of love and light. We all come from this love and light field, and therefore, we can simply realign with our origins or the origins of a certain emotion or situation, whereby we will find that the origin is one of love and light.

The third definition is recreating lovingly and lightly. Let's say someone made fun of you in kindergarten. The most common response to this is to feel shame or inadequacy. In this context, recreating lovingly and lightly could mean imagining the person apologizing and saying he or she didn't mean it. It could also mean recreating your response to that of "I know my worth, and I am enough." Recreating lovingly and lightly could be anything from recreating the situation in question and altering it so that something else in fact happened perceptually in your mind to recreating your response to the situation. However, your perception of the situation changes. As shown in the previous example, you might say you are leaving a situation of someone making fun of you with the perception that you know your worth and you are enough.

Reharmonizing lovingly and lightly is the fourth definition. Let's say you just had a fight with your boyfriend. In this context, we think about bringing a certain harmony back to your relationship: the harmony of love and light. This fourth definition generally applies to again harmonizing a relationship/situation that was already harmonious before. When using transmutation in this context, the love and light field just knows which definition or definitions to apply.

Notice that three of those four definitions involve "re": realigning, recreating, reharmonizing. That is because the premise is that everything originates lovingly and lightly. When they are born, babies have no concept of shame, guilt, or any other lower vibrations. Sure, they cry, but notice how in flow they are. As Marisa Peer said, "When babies are small and everybody looks at them, they don't put their hands over their face, saying, "Don't look at me. I'm having a bad hair day." No, a baby is in peace. In appreciation. In beauty. "Look at me. I am beautiful."

To recap, transmutation is

1. transforming into love and light.
2. realigning with love and light.
3. recreating lovingly and lightly.
4. reharmonizing lovingly and lightly.

Now imagine exiting your body and having a birds'-eye view of yourself. Study yourself. How are you sitting? Are you smiling or are you serious? Are you sitting cross-legged or are your feet straight on the floor? Now imagine dusting yourself with a transmutation powder and saying "I transmute you! I transmute you! I transmute you!"

Now enter your body in full force and declare this with all your energy: "I transmute all that I am. I transmute all that I have been! I transmute all that I will be! I transmute all my allignments! I transmute myself!"

Did that feel great or what! I would like you to do this with transmutations daily in your thoughts as an experiment for thirty days. Chant in your head, *I transmute. Any bad memory, I transmute that. Any bad situation, I transmute it. Any feeling, I transmute it.* Eventually, you will feel the light feeling of floating, that ease and grace. I guarantee it.

Another option is to do a daily transmutation ritual,

a dance, for example. Every morning as you get out of bed, put on your favorite song and do the transmutation dance while chanting "All this transmuted, all my vibrations transmuted, all my life transmuted."

Another ritual could be to write transmutations in different forms in a journal for five minutes each day. You could combine it with "I am so thankful and grateful":

I am so grateful and thankful that I am transmuted. I am so grateful and thankful that my whole life is transmuted. I am so grateful and thankful that every thought I have is transmuted. I am so grateful and thankful that every origin of every thought I have is transmuted. I am so thankful and grateful that every consequence of every thought I have is transmuted. I am so thankful and grateful that every feeling I have is transmuted. I am so thankful and grateful that every origin and every consequence of every feeling I have is transmuted. I am so thankful and grateful that every decision I make is transmuted. I am so thankful and grateful that every decision I will ever make is transmuted.

You can transmute anything and everything. Each day you may be inspired to transmute the same thing or something different. As long as you stay committed to transmuting each day, it doesn't matter.

Another ritual could be to paint TRANSMUTATION on a sign and hang it in the corner of your room. Each morning pray in front of that little corner:

Dear God,

> May my whole life be transmuted.
> May I be transmuted.
> May my vibrational alignments be transmuted.
> May the whole room be transmuted.
> May the whole house be transmuted.
> May the whole planet be transmuted.
> May my energy field be transmuted.
> May my friends' energy fields be transmuted.
> May my familiy's energy field be transmuted.
> May my friends' families' energy fields be transmuted.
> May we all be transmuted.

Then add the following: "Thank you, higher power. Thank you, God. Thank you, source. Thank you, universe. Thank you, life. Thank you, omniverse. Thank you, the entirety of all there is. Thank you, planet Earth. Thank you, humanity. Thank you, nature!"

Now breathe in and out.

Would you be willing to do one of these rituals now, starting today?

CHAPTER 9

SENDING LOVE AND COMPASSION AROUND THE WORLD

FROM TIME TO TIME, IT is important to connect to yourself, filling yourself with love and compassion by thinking about a kid, a pet, or a parent you hold close to your heart. Send that dear one love and compassion. Then send your whole environment love and compassion, then your workplace, then your friends and family, then your loving and light team, and then the whole planet.

Afterward, you can refill with love and compassion by thinking about a dear one and sending it to our whole star system. Moreover, to our whole galaxy. Moreover, to our whole universe. Moreover, to our whole divine order and God, source, and Creator. Filling yourself and the world with love is a great act of courage that is worth your having a great contribution in the world. Many meditation teachers teach by sending the world and themselves love and compassion, and I agree with this teaching profoundly.

Simply start by shifting your brain chemistry by filling it with love. You will be filled with feel-good hormones and neurotransmitters such as endorphins. You will feel great. On top of that, you will contribute to the world's shifting for the better a small bit a day. Each extra day you send love and compassion, you and the world willl feel better too.

CHAPTER 10

TAKING RESPONSIBILITY FOR YOURSELF

IN THIS CHAPTER, I WILL cover what actually taking responsibility looks like.

About five years ago, I was very angry with God. I felt as if everyone would be a good person, a good entity, a good creator, and good at whatever as long as they were happy. I was blaming God for people around the world suffering and being in pain while at the same time I was sending light to my demons, who kept giving me death threats, and I thought it was unfair of him that he ever allowed anyone to be feeling unwell.

I remembered a quote by Vishen Lakhiani: "Hurt people hurt people." I thought that if God could just make sure everyone was well, there wouldn't be people in such pain that they would threaten other human beings or kill them. All the criminals and wars would just disappear if people would suffer less. I was fighting with God and blaming God, until I realized something … If it is in my reality, I either have to accept it or change it. I can't play the blame game. I am responsible for myself fully. In fact, I believe in such a responsibility of myself to the extent that I am responsible for anything that shows up in my world. Therefore, I started blessing every newspaper, every TV show, and every voice, thinking, *If it reaches me, I have to do something about it.* Helped by the book *Ho'oponopono*, I even knew that the least I could do was, connected to oneness, say "I'm sorry, please forgive me, thank you, and I love you" in every thought.

A friend of mine who had just gone through a divorce visited me, and to this day, she says it was a miracle how much better she felt after talking to me. When I told her my secret of the four sentences, the healing prayer of Ho'oponopono in my head, she said, confused, "Whatever you did when we spoke, it worked."

I call this being responsible for every thought, action, result, and alignment. Everything I go along with, even if by mistake, I am responsible for. Therefore, I have the power to change it or accept it. Remember: there is no guilt here. Being responsible for something does not mean feeling guilty. Just connect to love and light and take responsibility without any guilt. If guilt pops up, just remember that at the time when you felt guilty about what happened, you simply didn't know better. You can release the guilt and take responsibility. Being responsible for oneself makes for a much better and more enjoyable life than blaming yourself or others.

CHAPTER 11

MEDITATION

DO YOU THINK IT'S IMPORTANT to meditate daily? I certainly do.

I will list a few meditations you can start with immediately.

1. Shower or bath meditation: Visualize yourself having a shower of light each day—or a pink one or a golden one. As you clean your physical body, imagine cleansing your spiritual and emotional one as well. Imagine bathing in a light glowing water and cleansing yourself from all negative energies, thinking beautiful thoughts such as I love myself.

2. Walking meditation: As you walk, connect to the earth and ground yourself in her core filled with light. Feel each step you take. Look around

youat what you see. This is a type of mindfulness meditation.

3. Other mindfulness meditations can be done by breathing in and out throughout your day or when you eat, really enjoying the taste of the food. As you take each bite, taste the food, smell it, pay attention to its texture, and hear the sounds around you as you eat. Also, one way is to burn a candle in front of you and stare at it as it burns, noticing the lights, colors, smells, and heat.

4. There are mantra-based mediations where you take fifteen to twenty minutes a day to repeat "Om" or "One" in your head or aloud. Another mantra you can repeat is "love, love love. Light, light, light. God, God, God." You can replace God with any higher power such as Nature, Source, highest self. This is a great mantra.

5. Guided meditations: These can be for different purposes, such as enhancing your intuition, gaining confidence, or talking to your guides.

6. The easiest and best meditations I do daily are the relaxation ones, where you relax your whole body from scalp to feet. Then relax your mind by visualizing yourself on the beach or in a forest or

mountain area. After a few minutes of this, you start giving yourself positive belief systems, such as my mentor José Silva's personal favorite: "Every day, in every way, I am getting better better and better."

7. Gratitude meditations: Relax, and connect to what you are truly grateful for, even simply that you have drinkable water available. Keep expanding the gratitude energy and adding things from the future that you are grateful for, as if you already have them.

8. Love and compassion meditation: Send love and compassion to yourself and the world. Connect to someone you truly love and to source from above and below. You do this by imagining a light coming from up above in the sky either the heavens or the galactic sun and you imagine the light going through you into the ground and deep into the center of the earth connecting to the light there. Then you bring back the light into you, exchanging the energies from deep in the earth and up above and as they pass through you you activate your heart center by picturing a loved one. Then you send that I love you energy to your

loved one and all your friends, family, enemies, everyone you can think of including the earth and the universe.

9. Manifesting or active meditatations. These are typically also guided meditations. You can manifest a better connection to your guides, a better connection to your higher self, a better connection to God and a better connection to your soul. These are good places to start when manifesting and from there you know that everything you manifest afterward is good for you. Then you can actively direct your mind to whatever you want.

10. You can also actively engage in forgiveness meditations everyday. Forgiveness of yourself and others. Forgiveness is a gift you give to yourself. You feel better and lighter afterwards and it just leads to a happier life.

11. Monastic meditations (typically done by monks who sit in silence all day)

CHAPTER 12

YOUR PERSONAL MISSION AND THE MISSION OF YOUR LOVING AND LIGHT TEAM

LET ME START THIS CHAPTER with an example: "My personal mission is to heal the world, make it a better place, enjoy right now, play, have fun, and rest." After you find your personal mission through the original loving and light team that is given to you, a good place to start is to ask your thoughts or vibration, "Who would like to be a part of my mission?"

That's how you find your lifetime loving and light team, the ones that believe in you and your mission.

So who would like to heal the world, make it a better place, enjoy right now, have fun, play, and rest?

As the loving and light field works through you, you gain awareness and insight, and with time you connect to your own purpose and mission and those people, angels, and entities that believe in your mission come to you. The right team just flows to you, each with its unique speciality.

Printed in the United States
By Bookmasters